Pocket Guide to
CIGARS

M. Shanken Communications, Inc.
NEW YORK

9   8   7   6   5   4   3   2   0
Digit on the right indicates the number of this printing

ISBN 1-881659-87-9

Interior Art Direction by Chandra Hira
Interior Design by Cheryl McGovern

For subscriptions to CIGAR AFICIONADO magazine go to:
www.cigaraficionado.com

Since the first edition of this little guide was published, the cigar renaissance has mushroomed beyond even my wildest expectations.

In the surge of antismoking fervor that began in the 1970s, cigar smokers suffered harassment and inconvenience far beyond reason. Restrictions sprang up everywhere: "Smoking Section. No pipes or cigars allowed" was common on menus and restaurant walls. By the early 1990's, the remaining devotees of premium hand-rolled cigars were condemned to second-class citizenship.

With the launch of CIGAR AFICIONADO in 1992, everything changed. The small coterie of passionate cigar lovers suddenly had a voice, a forum to express the truth about its favorite pastime: that cigars are one of life's truly great pleasures. At the same time, cigar makers began to respond to the demand for full-flavored, rich-tasting cigars. Tobacconists introduced new and improved products. Attracted by the lure of sophisticated pleasure, new smokers—especially young men in their late 20s and 30s, and some women, too—joined the fun. Celebrities who had hidden their enjoyment of cigars stepped forward to publicly announce that they, too, loved a great smoke.

The change has been astonishing. *Cigar Aficionado's Pocket Guide* is your perfect introduction to the world of cigars. Learn how to differentiate cigars by size, shape, color, strength and country of origin. What's the best way to cut a cigar? Single blade? Double blade? Should you light your cigar with a match or a lighter? Do you need to store your cigars? This handy guide will tell you how. Plus, you'll get answers to cigar smokers' most frequently asked questions.

The cigar is here to stay. Enjoy it.

Marvin R. Shanken
Editor & Publisher, *Cigar Aficionado*

BILL MILNE

Contents

The Western world first learned of tobacco shortly after Christopher Columbus dropped anchor off the Cuban coast in October, 1492. Two of the men he sent ashore reported back that they had seen natives with "smoking heads." Columbus brought tobacco seeds back to Europe, and within 80 years, this New World plant was in widespread use throughout the Old World.

It's fitting that Cuban tobacco was the first to be exported, for even now the Cuban product is considered by many—particularly lovers of hand-rolled, premium cigars—to be the finest available. Today tobacco is grown in many parts of the world, with the dark tobacco used in quality cigars found mainly in three tropical areas: Latin America and the Caribbean; near the South China Sea in East Asia; and West Africa.

Because tobacco is genetically stable—that is, the seeds of tobacco plants remain genetically pure from one generation to the next—you might expect that Cuban-seed tobacco grown in the Dominican

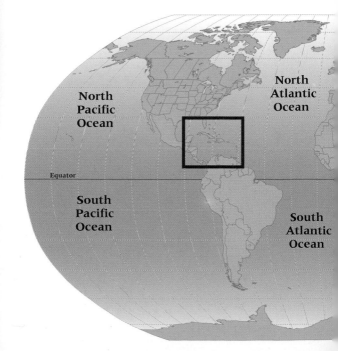

North Pacific Ocean

North Atlantic Ocean

Equator

South Pacific Ocean

South Atlantic Ocean

Republic would taste identical to that grown from the same strain of seed in Cuba itself. But this is not the case. Like wine grapes, tobacco plants are affected by variations in soil and climate. These variations can produce differences—striking or subtle—in the taste of the final product.

Cuba

Perhaps the best tobacco-growing region in the world is the Vuelta Abajo, which comprises most of Pinar del Rio, the westernmost province of Cuba. About 100,000 acres of the rich, red soil here are planted with cigar tobacco, but the best of all comes from a small area near the towns of San Juan y Martinez and San Luis. Plantations well-known for their wrapper leaves include Laguira and El Corojo ("The Wrapper"), while Hoyo de Monterrey specializes in filler tobacco.

Small *vegas* (plantations) of up to 150 acres are privately owned, while larger ones belong to the government. Each plantation's tobacco is sold at fixed prices to one or more of the government-run cigar factories in Havana; each factory, in turn, may produce

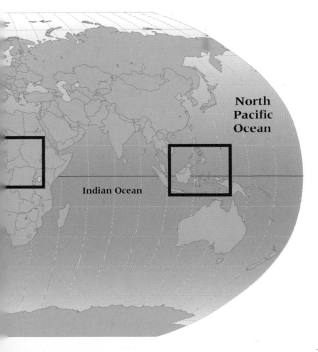

North Pacific Ocean

Indian Ocean

several brands, either for export or for domestic consumption. Several other areas of Cuba are devoted to tobacco cultivation as well. The Semi-Vuelta, also in Pinar del Rio, specializes in filler tobacco; so does Remedios, in the central part of the island, whose product is used mainly for blending. The tobacco grown in Oriente, in the southeast, is of somewhat lesser quality, and is used in cigars destined for the local market.

Probably the best tobacco region after the Vuelta Abajo is Partido, just southwest of Havana. Traditionally, Partido specialized in the green wrapper leaves known as candela; now that green cigars are out of favor on the world market, the area is experimenting, quite successfully, with Connecticut-seed wrappers.

Dominican Republic

When the United States embargoed all Cuban products in 1962, following Fidel Castro's revolution, the largest market for Havanas suddenly evaporated. Cigar manufacturing firms—some of them American-owned—began to look elsewhere for land that could produce fine tobacco. They found it in Cuba's Caribbean neighbor, the Dominican Republic.

This island nation is now the world's largest producer of handmade premium cigars, and its output continues to grow. More than 18,000 acres of tobacco were planted for the 1996 crop, 50 percent more than the previous year. Several types of filler tobacco are grown here; *piloto Cubano*, for example, whose seed originated in Cuba's Vuelta Abajo, is noted for its richness and intensity, while *olor* has a more neutral flavor. The types are mixed together in varying proportions to produce distinctive blends.

The best tobacco-growing region of the Dominican Republic is the six-mile-wide Yaque Valley, which extends from the city of Santiago (in the north central part of the country) about 25 miles northwest to the town of Esperanza. Approximately 4,500 tiny tobacco farms dot the area. Some farmers have contracts with specific manufacturers, but most sell to middlemen called *empacadores* (packers), who process the tobacco before selling it to cigar producers.

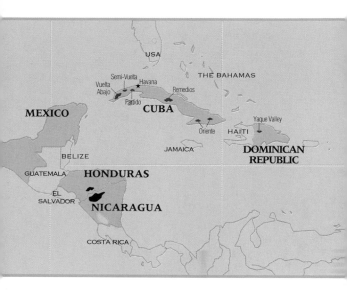

Honduras and Nicaragua

These two Central American nations share a common border—and a common history of troubled tobacco industries in the 1980s.

In Honduras, the problem was disease. Honduran cigar tobacco is almost exclusively Cuban-seed in origin, a fact that the country's cigar makers point to proudly when claiming that their product tastes more like a true Havana than any other in the world. But Cuban-seed tobacco is especially subject to infestations of blue mold, which can destroy a tobacco field virtually overnight. In the mid-1980s, when the plague was at its height, the reputation of Honduras' famously strong, rich-tasting cigars suffered as some were made with inferior tobacco. But growers have since found new ways to battle the mold, and the industry is on the rebound.

Nicaragua's cigar industry is centered around the towns of Jalapa and Estelí in the northwestern part of the country near the Honduran border. And in the 1980s, geography was destiny: it was precisely this area that was the scene of the heaviest fighting between Sandinista government forces and the U.S.-backed Contras throughout the country's 10-year-long civil war. Tobacco fields were mined, and curing barns were used as military barracks by both sides. The industry suffered major setbacks, but since the mid-1990s it

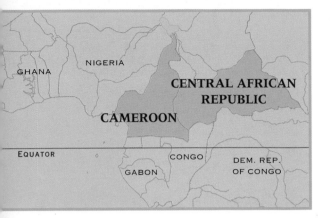

has come roaring back; in fact, in 1996, Nicaragua leapt ahead of Jamaica and Mexico to become the third largest exporter of cigars to the United States (after the Dominican Republic and Honduras).

Mexico

The state of Veracruz, on the southern curve of Mexico's Gulf coast, is home to this country's two tobacco-growing regions. Filler tobacco and a native black *tabaco negro* used for maduro wrappers grow in the northern part of the state. Maduro wrappers are grown in the south as well, specifically in the San Andres Valley, but here the specialty is a strain of Sumatra-seed tobacco used in both binders and wrappers. The Sumatra-seed wrapper leaves are prized for their silkiness and delicate vein structure.

Ecuador

This South American country is best known for its high-quality wrapper leaves, both shade- and sun-grown. Both Sumatra-seed and Connecticut-seed varieties are used to produce wrappers that are silky to the touch and have great visual appeal as well, due to their excellent colors and very light vein structure.

Brazil

Most Brazilian cigar tobacco is of the local Mata Fina variety, which grows in the Bahia region on the central east coast. Frequently used as filler in premium cigars, Mata Fina is a dark, richly flavored tobacco with a touch of sweetness. The other native Brazilian tobacco, Arapiraca, comes from Alagoas, just north of Bahia. It is not widely used today, because of its lack of distinctive flavor.

Connecticut

This New England state is the major exception to the rule that premium cigar tobacco grows only in tropical areas. The Connecticut River Valley north of Hartford produces one of the finest wrappers in the world: Connecticut Shade. The golden tan, finely textured leaves have a high degree of elasticity and a mild- to medium-bodied taste. Another type grown here, Connecticut Broadleaf, is a sun-grown tobacco used mainly for dark maduro wrappers; it is thicker and more heavily veined than shade-grown.

Cameroon/Central African Republic

A high-quality, Sumatra-seed leaf known as Cameroon wrapper is grown in both of these West African nations. Greenish-brown to dark brown in color, Cameroon leaf has a unique grain called "tooth"; it is prized for its pleasant yet neutral flavor characteristics, which make it an ideal wrapper for full-flavored tobaccos. Management difficulties and bad weather have led to decreased production in recent years.

Indonesia and the Philippines

The archipelago of Indonesia is the source of the wrapper leaf known as Sumatra-seed (or Java-seed), which is now grown in a number of places around the world. Actual Sumatra-grown wrapper tobacco is usually dark brown in color and neutral in flavor; the majority is used in the manufacture of small cigars. The Philippines, Indonesia's neighbor to the northeast, produces a hybrid strain of cigar tobacco that is mild in flavor but very aromatic.

Making a hand-rolled cigar is a complicated art. Experienced farmers, master blenders and skilled rollers are essential to the process, and they carry out the time-honored tradition of producing premium cigars with great pride.

Growing Tobacco

The cigar-making process begins in the tobacco fields. The varieties of tobacco that are used for cigar production—Connecticut-seed or Cuban-seed, for example—provide varying flavors and leaf sizes.

ANGELO CAVALLI

It takes anywhere from 80-90 days for a seed to develop into a full-grown plant that is ready for harvest.

BLEACHER & EVEREL

A worker inspects newly harvested tobacco leaves.

But in the field, tobacco is treated almost identically with one key distinction: whether it is sun- or shade-grown. Sun-grown tobacco is exposed to the full strength of the sun throughout the growing season. This makes for a more robust leaf with stronger flavors and darker colors. Shade-grown, normally reserved for wrapper leaves, is planted under a gauze-like tarp producing a more visually appealing, larger, thinner leaf with smaller veins.

The growing cycle is virtually identical for all cigar tobacco varieties. The seeds, the size of grains of sand, are germinated in a greenhouse and planted in raised seedbeds. It takes approximately six weeks for the plants to reach a height of six to eight inches. The strongest, healthiest plants with the most solid root structure are transplanted to the fields. Approximately 40 days after transplanting, the top part of the stalk is cut off. At 45 to 55 days, the first leaves, which practically lay on the ground, are removed and discarded. At the same time, the next row of leaves up—the leaves grow in concentric circles in groups of three up the stalk of the plant—is harvested; this is called the first priming.

- The first priming yields the lightest and sweetest of the plants' leaves, which are used for binder and some wrapper. They are known for their combustion qualities because they are so thin and papery.

- The second priming is harvested approximately seven days after the first priming. It also has a sweet quality but has more nicotine in it, which makes it stronger and more flavorful. A higher percentage of this priming is used for wrapper, but it is still primarily used for binders and fillers.

- The third priming yields the most elegant leaves on the plant, and up to 70 percent of them will be used for wrapper. They also have some sweetness and still higher percentages of nicotine, and are used to balance out filler blends.

Tobacco plants can grow up to 7 feet high. Forty days after a plant is transplanted in the field, the top part is cut off. Several days later, the lower leaves are harvested. This is called the *first priming*.

The tobacco leaves are tied together in bunches, then hung to dry before beginning the fermentation process.

- The fourth priming has much more body, due to more exposure to sunlight. The leaves from this level of the plant are richer and usually darker in color. While this tobacco begins to be heavier in texture, it is also used for wrapper.

- The fifth priming includes some of the most robust leaves on the plant, especially in the Cuban-seed variety. In general, less wrapper comes from this priming; most of it is used for binder and filler. But if you see a very dark-wrapped cigar that is not a maduro, it may very well come from the fifth priming. By now, the leaf requires extended fermentation and processing to lighten its texture and reduce its strength if it is to be used for a wrapper. Given their thicker texture, these leaves also don't burn as well.

- The sixth priming is usually used only for long filler. It has the heaviest texture and is slow-burning. But it is very flavorful. Some companies age sixth priming tobacco as much as five years before putting it into cigars. It is not suitable for wrappers because the leaves get smaller near the top of the plant.

After the plant has reached maturity, it is ready to be harvested. The exact timing for the harvesting depends on the weather and the farmer's experience in judging the ripeness of the tobacco. Seed variety is

The leaves dry in large wooden barns called casas de tabacos.

also a factor, as some seed varieties grow more quickly than others; it takes anywhere from 80 to 90 days for a seed to develop into a full-grown plant.

After being harvested, the cigar tobacco enters the fermentation stage. In this stage, the tobacco is slightly moistened, then piled in huge bales or stacks; temperatures inside the bales reach as high as 140°F as the tobacco "sweats" during the early stages of the fermentation. Some tobacco may be "turned" up to three or four times and remoistened before fermentation finally ceases. The process releases ammonia from the tobacco and reduces overall nicotine content.

The fermented tobacco is then wrapped in bales— usually surrounded by burlap—to age. Standard aging time is 18 months to two years, although some manufacturers keep inventories of tobacco as old as 10 years. The tobacco is then slightly dampened again to make it supple before being turned over to the rollers.

Making the Cigar

A cigar blend is created by a master blender, someone who combines tobaccos of varying tastes and strengths to create a balanced, harmonious smoke. Depending on its ring gauge, a cigar will contain a blend of between two and four different tobaccos. Each type of tobacco leaf is placed in different boxes at the roller's desk, and the roller is given the formula for the specific cigar he or she is making.

The roller takes the leaves and presses them together in his hand; he then places the leaves on a binder leaf—a flat, somewhat elastic leaf of tobacco—to hold it together. He rolls them together into a "bunch," cuts them to the appropriate length and then places them in the bottom half of a wooden mold. After he puts the upper half of the mold in place, he puts the entire box into a screw press. The press operator will usually break down the press once, turn the bunch inside the mold and then rebox and press the bunch again, for a total pressing time of about an hour.

The cigar rollers follow a formula created by a master blender when crafting each cigar.

Cigar rollers can produce from 100 to 150 cigars a day, using only a wooden board, metal knife and small guillotine as well as a bit of glue.

Once the worker has pressed the cigar, he returns the wooden molds to the rolling tables. The roller removes the bunch and wraps it with the wrapper leaf, a supple, very elastic and visually beautiful leaf that has been cut in half. Keeping constant pressure on the bunch and the wrapper, the cigar maker rolls the leaf around the bunch and applies a bit of vegetable glue to bond the wrapper leaf together at the head so the cigar won't unravel.

Supervisors inspect each cigar by hand. They feel it for weight and for any hard spots, which could indicate a plug, or soft spots, which can cause an uneven burn. They reject defective cigars. Then, in most factories, workers weigh the cigars in bunches of 50. Good cigar makers will have less than 1 gram of variation between 50-cigar bunches. Bunches with significant weight variations may be returned to the roller.

Aging the Cigar

The next stop for cigars is the aging room. Most factories age their cigars a least 21 days, and some leave them in the aging room for anywhere from 90 to 180 days. This allows the different cigar tobaccos to "marry" and create a more balanced smoke. After aging, the cigars are selected for each box, checked for fine gradations in wrapper leaf color, and finally, packed in boxes for shipping.

Cigar box size varies, but typically a box holds 25 or 50 cigars.

After packaging, the cigars are aged again—for anywhere from 3 weeks to 6 months—before shipping.

igar sizes have two dimensions: length (in either inches or centimeters) and ring gauge, a measurement divided into 64ths of an inch (or, in the European method, millimeters). A cigar with a ring gauge of 40, for example, measures 40/64th of an inch in diameter.

Cigar shapes are divided into two categories: *parejos*, which are the familiar cigars with straight sides, a closed head (the end you smoke), and an open foot (the end you light); and *figurados*, which include all irregularly-shaped cigars.

Please note that names for specific sizes and shapes are *not* standardized from brand to brand. The dimensions listed below represent an average or typical example of each format.

Parejos (Straight-Sided Cigars)
Churchill: A large corona format. The traditional dimension is 7 inches by a 48 ring.

Churchill   Corona   Corona Gorda   Double Corona

Corona: The traditional proportion is 5 1/2 to 6 inches with a ring gauge of 42 to 44.

Corona Gorda: This long robusto format could be called a robusto extra, although its popularity preceded that of robustos. The traditional measurements are 5 5/8 inches by a 46 ring.

Double Corona: The standard dimension is 7 1/2 to 8 inches by a 49 to 52 ring.

Lonsdale: The classic size is 6 1/4 inches by a 42 to 44 ring.

Panetela: More popular in years past than today. This thin format varies more widely in length than almost any other cigar size, from 5 to 7 1/2 inches and from a 34 to 38 ring gauge.

Petit Corona: This short corona is usually 4 1/2 inches by a 40 to 42 ring gauge.

Robusto: This short Churchill format is growing in popularity. The traditional size is 5 to 5 1/2 inches by a 50 ring gauge.

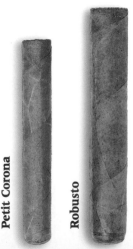

JEFF HARRIS

Lonsdale

Panetela

Petit Corona

Robusto

21

Figurados

Belicoso: Traditionally, a belicoso was a short pyramid, 5 or 5 1/2 inches in length with a shorter, more rounded taper at the head and a ring gauge generally of 50 or less. Today, belicosos are frequently coronas or coronas gordas with a tapered head.

Culebra: This most exotic shape is actually three panatelas braided together and banded as one cigar. You smoke them separately. They are usually 5 to 6 inches in length, most often with a 38 ring gauge. Culebras are hard to come by today.

Diademas: A true torpedo. The head and foot on this cigar are both closed. It is usually 8 inches or longer and is often boxed individually. It has a ring gauge of 40 at the head and 52 to 54, or even larger, at the foot.

Perfecto: This cigar is closed at both ends. The head is rounded, not tapered. The foot is closed like a torpedo or a diademas. It is usually shaped with a bulge

Belicoso   Culebra   Diademas

in the middle. Perfectos can vary greatly in length, from 4 1/2 to 9 inches and can have a ring gauge between 38 and 48.

Pyramid: A tapered-head cigar with an open foot (the end you light). These cigars are between 6 and 7 inches with a ring gauge of around 40 at the head that widens to between 52 and 54 at the foot. The difference between a pyramid and a torpedo is that the pyramid's foot is cut, whereas the torpedo has a closed foot.

Color

Double Claro or Candela

Claro

Colorado Claro or Natural

Colorado

Colorado Maduro

Maduro

Oscuro

Perfecto

Pyramid

By Country with Strength Designation

The cigar brands below are grouped by country of origin. A heading such as "Honduras & Nicaragua" indicates that the same manufacturer makes the same brand in two different countries.

However, because of trademark disputes between the Cuban government and those who owned Cuban brands prior to Castro's revolution—and who have since established factories elsewhere—you will see some brand names listed twice, under Cuba and another country as well. These are *not* the same cigar. For example, note that the Cuban Hoyo de Monterrey has a strength designation of E (strong), while the Honduran Hoyo de Monterrey is designated C (medium).

The relative strength designations represent an average strength for each brand. There may be some variation among the different lines within each brand.

Key: Relative Strength

A. Mild
B. Mild to Medium
C. Medium
D. Medium to Strong
E. Strong

Bahamas

Graycliff: C
Graycliff Crystal: D
Graycliff Espresso: D

Cuba

Bolivar: D
Cohiba: E
Cuaba: D
Diplomaticos: C
El Rey del Mundo: B/C
Flor de Rafael Gonzalez: D
Fonseca: C
H. Upmann: D
Hoyo de Monterrey: D/E
José Piedra: B
Juan Lopez: D
Montecristo: C/D
Partagas: D/E
Punch: E
Quai d'Orsay: C
Ramon Allones: D
Romeo y Julieta: D
Saint Luis Rey: D
San Cristobal de la Habana: C/D
Sancho Panza: D
Trinidad: D
Vegas Robaina: D
Vegueros: C

Dominican Republic

Arturo Fuente Añejo: C/D
Ashton: B

Ashton Aged Maduro: B

Ashton Heritage Puro Sol: B

Ashton Virgin Sun Grown: D/E

Aurora: B

Aurora 100 Años: D

Aurora Preferidos: C/D

Avo: B

Avo Maduro: B

Avo Signature: D

Avo XO: C

Bauzá: C

Black Pearl: C

Butera: C

Cacique: C

Carlos Toraño Exodus 1959: C

Casa Blanca Reserve: B

Cohiba: C

Cubita: B

Cubita Spanish Market Selection: C

Cuesta-Rey: B

Cuesta-Rey Centro Fino Sungrown: C

Cusano 10th Anniversary: C

Cusano 18 Double Connecticut: B

Cusano Corojo Vintage 1997: C

Davidoff: A/B

Davidoff Millennium Blend Series: C/D

Diablo: C

Diamond Crown: A

Diamond Crown Maximus: C

Domaine Avo: C

Don Diego Aniversario: C

Don Tomás: C

Dunhill signed range: B

El Rico Habano: D

Felipe Gregorio: C

Fonseca: A

Fonseca Sun Grown Cedar: B

Fonseca Vintage: B

Fuente Fuente OpusX: E

H. Upmann: B

H. Upmann Vintage Cameroon: C

H. Upmann 2000: C

H. Upmann Chairman's Reserve: B

Havana Sun Grown: C

Henry Clay: B

Independencia: C

La Flor Dominicana 2000 Series: B

La Flor Dominicana Double Ligero: D/E

La Flor Dominicana Ligero: D

La Flor Dominicana Maduro: C

La Flor Dominicana Reserva Especial: A

La Gloria Cubana: C/D

La Gloria Cubana Serie R: D

La Gloria Cubana Reserva Figurados: C

La Unica: B

León Jimenes: B

Leoninos: B

Litto Gomez Diez: E

Macanudo Café: A

Macanudo Gold Label: A

Macanudo Maduro: B

Macanudo Robust: B

Macanudo Vintage: B

Montecristo: A

Montecristo Platinum Series: C

Montecristo Serie V: D

Montecristo White: A

Montesino: B

Occidental Reserve Double Maduro: C

Onyx Reserve: C
Padilla Connecticut: B
Padilla Hybrid Blend: C
Padilla Maduro: B
Partagas: B
Partagas Black Label: B
Partagas Cifuentes Blend: C
Partagas Limited Reserve: C
Partagas Spanish Rosado: C
Paul Garmirian: B
Playboy by Don Diego: B
Ramon Allones: C
Romeo y Julieta 1875: B
Romeo y Julieta
Aniversario: C
Romeo y Julieta Reserve
Maduro: C
Romeo y Julieta Vintage: C
Royal Jamaica: B
Royal Jamaica Gold: C
Savinelli E.L.R. B
Sosa: B
The Griffin's: A
The Griffin's Fuerte: B
Trinidad: C
Trinidad Maduro: D
V Centennial: C
Vegas de Fonseca: C
Zino Platinum
Crown Series: B
Zino Platinum
Scepter Series: B

Honduras

Ancient Warrior: B
Astral: B
Bolivar Fuerte: D
C.A.O. Brazilia: C
C.A.O. Italia: C
C.A.O. MX2: C
Camacho: C
Camacho Corojo: D
Camacho Special
Limited Reserve: D
Carlos Toraño Exodus
1959 Silver: C

Casa Toraño: A
Cienfuegos: C
Conga Black Pearl: C
Cosmo: B
Cuba Aliados: C
Don Melo Centenario: D
Don Tomás: C
El Rey del Mundo: D
Flor de Copan: C
Flor del Caribe: B
Gispert: B
Gran Habano: B/C
Gurkha: C
Helix: A
Helix Maduro: B
Hoyo de Monterrey
Excalibur 1066: C
Hoyo de Monterrey
Excalibur: B
Hoyo de Monterrey
Dark Sumatra: C
Hoyo de Monterrey
Excalibur Royal Sterling: C
Indian Tabac: B/C
K. Hansotia & Co.
Symphony: B
La Aroma de Cuba: C
Maria Guerrero: B
Peterson Gran Reserva: D
Punch: C/D
Punch Gran Puro: C
Punch Rare Corojo: C
Puros Indios: C
Rocky Patel Sun Grown: C
Rocky Patel Vintage: C
Saint Luis Rey: C
Sancho Panza: B

Mexico
Te-Amo: C/D
Te-Amo Aniversario: C

Nicaragua
Bahia: B/C
Black Pearl: C
Bucanero: B

C.A.O. L'Anniversaire 1968-1998 Cameroon: C

C.A.O. L'Anniversaire extreme: C

C.A.O. 65th Anniversary: C/D

C.A.O. Criollo: B

C.A.O. Gold: C

Carlos Toraño 1916 Cameroon: C

Carlos Toraño Nicaragua Selection: C

Centenario: C

Condega Cuban Seed Corojo 1999: C

Cuban Parejo: C

Don Lino Africa: D

Edición de Silvio: B

Felipe Gregorio: C

Flor de Oliva 10th Anniversary: C

Jericho: B/C

Joya de Nicaragua Antaño 1970: E

Joya de Nicaragua Celebración: B

Juan Lopez: D

La Finca: C

La Tradicion Perdomo Reserve: C

La Vieja Habana C

Nicarao: C

Oliva Master Blends: B

Oliva "O" Bold: D

OneOff: C/D

OneOff Allegria: C

Padrón: C

Padrón 1964 Anniversary Series: C

Padrón Serie 1926: D

Perdomo Estate Selección: C

Perdomo2: C

Petrus: C

Pryme Limited Edition Gold Series: B

Savinelli Fuerte: D

Trilogy Ovation Corojo: C

XXO: C

USA

Flor de Gonzalez Reserva Selecta: C

La Gloria Cubana: C

Padilla Miami Blend: C

Tatuaje: D

Cutters

There are many acceptable ways to cut a cigar, but a double-edged guillotine cutter is perhaps the best way to prepare a cigar for smoking. Place the cigar firmly between the two blades, and clip the head off with a decisive stroke. The double-blade mechanism applies equal pressure to both sides of the cigar, providing the cleanest cut possible with very little damage to the cigar. It opens the entire head of the cigar, which allows for a smooth, even flow of smoke.

A single-blade guillotine achieves the same kind of open-ended cut. With a single blade, however, the cutting edge presses against only one side of the cigar and can distort its shape, sometimes rupturing or tearing the wrapper.

A scissors also creates an open-ended cut. Unless the scissors is sharp, perfectly balanced and appropriately sized for your hand, it is very hard to get the necessary leverage and stability needed for a clean cut. Also, a scissors is usually less portable than a guillotine cutter. Another popular cutter is the wedge or V-cutter, which leaves a deep V-shaped gouge in the cigar. But if you chew your cigar, the wedge cutter may not be for you. As you moisten the cut edges of the V, they may collapse. Tars will accumulate in the now narrow opening, making the cigar taste harsh.

An auger, a drill or a piercer will punch a hole in one end of the cigar. However, this concentrates the smoke into a single aperture, where—as in a collapsed V-cut—tars may build up, creating a harsh smoke.

Using your teeth is acceptable if you don't have any other cutting device. Try to use the same principle as that of a double-edged guillotine—press your teeth against both sides of the cigar and bite firmly.

ANITA CALERO

Lighters

Once you cut the cigar, the next task is to light it.
Regardless of the method you select, there are some
basic rules. Never let the flame actually touch the
cigar. Instead, rotate the cigar slightly above the
flame tip so that you light the entire foot of the cigar.
Blow through the cigar after embers appear on the
end to expel any odors that may have come from the
lighter or match.

Wooden matches remain one of the best ways to light
a cigar. Always let the sulfur burn off before bringing
the tip of the flame about 1/2 inch under the cigar's
foot. A wide flame is best; don't hesitate to use two or

ANITA CALERO

three matches at once to get a proper light. Small strips of cedar, called spills, are ideal for lighting cigars. But they can be inconvenient, as you must carry around little strips of wood as well as a lighter.

Butane lighters are perfectly acceptable. They burn with an even flame, and some lighters, made specifically for cigars, actually come with two burners to increase the size of the flame. The lighters often are windproof, and they are not only portable, but can be a beautiful piece of jewelry as well.

Some lighters are less than ideal. A fluid-fuel lighter must be used very carefully: If you pull the fumes through the cigar, they can affect the taste. But used properly, this type of lighter is perfectly functional.

Never light your cigar from a candle flame. The wax particles in the flame will ruin the taste of your cigar and make it burn less smoothly. And beware of anything other than wood that burns with a noticeable odor; the cigar could absorb these aromas, which would affect its taste.

Humidors and Travel Cases

Cigars must be kept in a properly humidified environment. The correct ambiance is 70 to 72 percent relative humidity and a temperature of 70°F. A sealed environment is required to keep both elements stable. Avoid large or rapid fluctuations in either temperature or humidity; they can swell the bunch and crack the wrapper.

Wooden desktop humidors with humidity regulators are usually more than adequate to keep cigars. Built in sizes to accommodate anywhere from 50 to about 500 cigars, they offer a controlled environment. Check the cigars weekly, however, to ensure that the humidor maintains them at a proper moisture level. As for temperature, as long as you don't place the humidor next to a radia-tor, the cigars should be OK; most home environments remain between 68°F and 72°F.

JEFF HARRIS

Large standing cabinet humidors, with capacities of up to 1,500 cigars, are now available. They may include both temperature and humidity controls, and they have enough shelf space to store cigars in their original wooden boxes—an essential for the serious connoisseur. With some modifications, you can also outfit a closet with the proper humidification and temperature controls and ideally, with Spanish cedar shelving—to create a walk-in humidor.

A cigar carrying case is an important accessory; it protects the cigars you take with you when you go out. Be sure to select a size that will accommodate your favorite cigar. And you may want more than one style: a four- or five-finger cigar holder is perfect for a day outdoors or a lengthy dinner party, while a two-finger model suffices for an after-dinner smoke with a friend—and fits in your pocket better.

Travel humidors are a separate category. They are built to hold anywhere from five to 25 cigars, and to fit easily in luggage or a briefcase. The humidification system will generally need recharging after two to five days of storage.

Dry Cigars

You discover a box of your favorite cigars that you left in a closet for six months, and they're as dry as a bone. What do you do?

First, have patience. Put the cigars in a humidor that hasn't been charged in the previous week. Let them rest in the slightly dry humidor for a few days so the cigars absorb a little humidity. Then, partially fill the humidification device; let the cigars rest for another week before charging it fully. This process will prevent the cigars from getting too much humidity too soon. If you shock the cigars with too much moisture, they may burst (split the wrapper).

JEFF HARRIS

If you have a cabinet-style humidor, first place the cigars as far as possible from the humidification device. Move them closer to the humidification device little by little over a period of six weeks.

In any case, do not light up until the cigars are supple to the touch. A dry cigar will burn too hotly, and the flavor will seem burned or carbonized.

The same principle applies to cold cigars or ones that have been kept frozen. (There's nothing wrong with this storage method except that the cigars don't age.) You must allow the cigars to return to normal temperature slowly. If you light them too soon, the abrupt change in temperature may cause them to crack open or explode. Give chilled cigars at least two or three days at the proper temperature in a humidified environment before lighting up.

10 Most Asked Questions About Cigars

In no particular order, here are answers to 10 of the most commonly asked questions about cigar smoking. If you're new to cigars, you will find this section invaluable, and if you've been smoking for years, you may learn some things you had not previously considered.

Q My cigars are overhumidified. What can I do to restore the humidor to optimal conditions? Can the cigars be saved?

A In most cases, the cigars can be saved. Overhumidification is a problem, especially prevalent during summer or in warmer, more sultry climates. But there are ways to combat it, and to ensure that your humidor stays in top shape year-round.

Adding cedar strips to the humidor – you'll find these in many cigar boxes – will help maintain optimum moisture levels. Put a strip or two on the bottom of the humidor, a strip in the middle, and another on top, and you'll watch the humidity reading drop as the cedar absorbs the humidor's extra moisture. Just keep an eye on the cigars, and add or remove cedar until you've reached the desired humidification.

The one thing you should not do is simply leave the lid of the humidor open — this can lead to wild fluctuations in humidity, and turn cigars that are too moist into dried-out cigars in a short time. Another thing to consider is the number of cigars in your humidor; if you have a very large box containing few cigars, the smokes may absorb more than their proper share of humidity.

Q I've noticed a powdery substance on several of my cigars. What is this, and need I be concerned?

A If the substance has a whitish color and can be easily dusted off the cigars without leaving residue, fear not. What you have in this case is "plume" (also called bloom), a natural occurrence caused by the cigars' sweating off some of the oils that are inherent to tobacco. Just dust off the cigars prior to smoking them.

If, however, the residue is more of a bluish color and leaves a stain on the wrapper when you dust it off, the cigars are the victims of mold. Mold is frequently caused by high temperature and humidity levels, so keeping your humidor near the optimal 70°F/70 percent humidity mark will help avoid this problem. Also, mold can be caused by not using distilled water in your humidification device, so know what sort of water you are using.

Q Although I generally use guillotine cutters, I was recently given a stylish wedge cutter. What's the difference, and will I damage my cigar?

A Wedge cutters were conceived decades ago, when the average cigar was much thinner than it is today. They were designed to open up a larger opening to chan-nel the smoke, which is

ALEXANDRA GRABLEWSKI

a consideration for lonsdales and coronas but generally not an issue for thicker cigars such as robustos. As a general rule, we prefer guillotines, as cigars cut with wedge cutters can accumulate tars that do not build up when using a straight cut. Also, wedge cutters tend to be imprecise in comparison with straight cutters, and you run the risk of damaging the cigar.

The third type of cutter that has become popular is the bullet, or lance, cutter. This type of cutter makes a circular hole in the head of the cigar, and it, too, has its drawbacks. First, it is easy to pierce the cigar too deeply, creating a tunnel near the head that makes the cigar burn hot. Also, as with a wedge cutter, the bullet hole left in the cigar's head allows tars to build up near the mouth of the smoker, frequently altering or souring the cigar's taste.

Q Occasionally some of my cigars will develop holes, and I've seen some small bugs crawling around my humidor. What should I do?

A Beetles cause one of the most devastating problems found in humidors because they can quickly decimate a cigar supply and are difficult to combat.

Beetle larvae are microscopic and occur naturally in tobacco, and, despite the quality control efforts of manufacturers, are frequently in cigars that make it to market. Once the temperature reaches 72°F, the beetles can hatch; they crawl through the cigars, creating those small round holes that essentially destroy a once-good smoke. But they can be combated by keeping a vigilant watch on your humidor's temperature, and perhaps by installing a beetle trap in your humidor. In addition, beetle larvae can be killed by freezing the cigars. Just put them in your freezer for three days, then move them into the fridge for one day. After you've frozen the cigars, though, take care to slowly acclimate them to rehumidification, lest the wrappers on the cigars crack.

Other bugs you may occasionally run into are wood mites—small, white insects that are often the result of opening a fresh wooden box of cigars. The good news is that these mites won't harm the cigars, and they don't live long enough to seriously damage your humidor.

Q My tobacconist sells many box-pressed cigars. Why do manufacturers do this? Is there an advantage to box-pressed smokes over round cigars?

A Box pressing is a stylistic decision, and it neither makes a cigar better nor worse than a round cigar. Lots of people favor the feel of a box-pressed smoke, and some manufacturers feel box pressing can correct potential construction flaws. But it is an aesthetic decision as to whether you prefer this style of cigar. Box pressing says nothing about the quality of the cigar, nor of the person who smokes it.

Q **What is the best way for me to age my cigars?**

A Many collectors choose to age their cigars in boxes, keeping like cigars together. Also, it's a good idea to age cigars at a slightly lower temperature and humidity level than normal, and then to move the aged smokes to a desktop humidor when you're ready to begin smoking them.

Many cigar brands, especially Cuban brands, are available in cabinet presentation, where the cigars are banded together with a ribbon in a format that makes them ideal for aging and long-term storage. While aging boxed cigars is certainly acceptable, these cabinet-packed smokes make even more attractive aging candidates, and therefore frequently command higher prices at auction.

Q **Many cigars are sold in individual cellophane overwraps. Should I remove the cellophane prior to placing the cigars in my humidor? What about tubes and bands? Are cigars best stored "naked"?**

ELIE BLEU

A Cellophane serves several purposes on a cigar—in states that require each cigar to have a warning label, it makes this notification much easier to accomplish, and it prevents damage to the cigars from excessive handling in cigar shops. But once you've bought the cigar and are placing it in your humidor, we recommend you remove the cellophane. Cellophane will prevent humidity from reaching the cigar, and you'll find the cigars will respond to humidification better if the overwrap has been removed. The same holds true for cigar tubes, whether glass or aluminum; these tubes will completely close off a cigar to humidification if left on. However, if you intend to transport your cigars (such as in a coat pocket), it may be a good idea to keep a few tubes or cellophane overwraps handy to protect the cigars during transport.

As far as bands are concerned, it's a matter of personal preference. Some people like to remove them, but when possible, we generally choose to keep the bands on (outside of our tasting procedures, of course). First, it makes identifying the cigars much easier, and it also prevents inadvertent damage to the cigar's wrapper that can occur while removing the band.

Q Can I use my Zippo lighter to light a cigar?

A It's probably not your best option. We suggest using wooden matches or, better yet, strips of cedar called spills. These will light your cigar without imparting to it the taste or odor of the oil found in lighter fluid. If you wish to use a lighter for your cigars, we recommend one that uses butane as its fuel, as these types of lighters are odorless. However, some smokers insist on using their old Zippo lighters, which may have sentimental value. If you're one of these people, just make sure that when lighting your cigar, the flame of the Zippo does not touch the cigar's foot. Once the cigar is lit, you may also choose to give the cigar one (and only one) outward puff, to clear it of any impurities caused by the lighter fluid.

Q My grandfather always dips his cigars in Cognac or rum. Is this a good idea? Why does my tobacconist warn me against it?

A Your grandfather probably started doing this decades ago, when cigars were shipped drier and humidification technology was not what it is today. Dipping the cigars in those years helped impart moisture to a dry cigar. Today, however, cigars are generally shipped and stored in optimally humidified conditions, and dipping a cigar in Cognac or rum will only serve to make your cigar soggy. What's more, the smoke will not taste like what it was dipped in, another reason we strongly recommend leaving the Cognac or rum in a glass, and enjoying it alongside your cigar.

Q I've been told you should only smoke a cigar halfway. Is this true? How can I tell when a cigar is done?

A The golden rule here is that a cigar is done whenever you're no longer enjoying it. But as a general maxim, we smoke our cigars about half to two-thirds of the way down. The reason is that a cigar gets hotter and more powerful the further down you smoke it, and its flavor changes as tars and moisture build up near the cigar's head. Smoke it too far, and you risk ruining the great flavor you've been enjoying. But this is simply a suggestion—if you're still enjoying the cigar as its lit end is about to burn your fingertips, go right on smoking it. Cigar smoking, after all, is about enjoyment.

JEFF HARRIS

Binder: The portion of a tobacco leaf used to hold together the "bunch," the blend of filler leaves inside the cigar.

Blend: The mixture of different types of tobacco in a cigar, including up to four types of filler leaves. Blending is an art, and blenders are responsible for brands keeping their signature taste from year to year.

Bloom: A naturally occurring phenomenon in the cigar aging process, also called plume, caused by the oils which are exuded during later fermentations. It appears as a fine, white powder and can be brushed off. Not to be confused with cigar mold, which is bluish in color and stains the wrapper.

Bouquet: The smell, or "nose," of a fine cigar. Badly-stored cigars lose their bouquet.

Box: Cigar boxes come in all shapes and sizes. Traditional styles include: *cabinet selection:* wood boxes with a sliding top designed to hold 25 or 50 cigars.

8-9-8: a round-sided box specifically designed to accommodate three rows of cigars—eight on top, nine in the middle, and eight on the bottom.

flat top, or 13-topper: a flat, rectangular box with 13 cigars on top and 12 on the bottom, divided by a spacer.

Bulk: A large pile of tobacco leaves in which fermentation occurs.

Bunch: The mass of up to four different types of filler tobacco that are blended and held together by the binder to form the body of a cigar.

Bundle: A packaging method, designed with economy in mind, that uses a cellophane overwrap. It usually contains 25 or 50 cigars, traditionally without bands. Seconds of premium brands are often sold in bundles.

Candela: A bright green shade of wrapper, achieved by a heat-curing process that fixes the chlorophyll content of wrapper leaves prior to fermentation. Also referred to as "double claro," or as American Market Selection (AMS).

Cap: A circular piece of wrapper leaf placed at the head of a cigar to secure the wrapper. A good cut will leave part of the cap intact.

Capa: The cigar's wrapper.

Chaveta: An oval-shaped blade used by rollers in cigar factories to cut wrapper leaves.

Cigar band: A ring of paper wrapped around the closed head of many cigars. Legend says that cigar bands were invented by Catherine the Great or by Spanish nobles to keep their gloves from being stained. Others credit their invention to a Dutchman named Gustave Bock, and state that the band helped keep the cigar wrapper together. Cigar bands are often printed with the name of the brand, country of origin, and/or indication that the cigar is hand-rolled. They also often have colorful graphics which have made them popular collectors' items. In many folktales, a cigar band serves as a wedding band in impromptu ceremonies. For the record, it is equally appropriate to leave the band on while smoking a cigar or to remove it, as long as the cigar's wrapper leaf is not torn when the band is removed.

Claro: A pale-green to light-brown shade of wrapper, characteristic of wrapper leaves grown in the shade.

Colorado: A medium-brown to brownish-red shade of wrapper leaf.

Double Claro: see Candela.

Draw: The amount of air that a smoker pulls through a lit cigar. A well-made cigar draws easily, yielding cool smoke. If the draw is too easy, the smoke will be too hot; if the cigar is plugged and the draw is tight, smoking it will not be relaxing.

Fermentation: Like fine wines, fine cigar tobaccos are the product of fermentation, and continue to go through additional stages of fermentation as they age. After the harvest, workers pile tobacco leaves into large "bulks," and moisten them to promote the primary fermentation. Temperatures inside a bulk may reach 140°F.

Figurado: A Spanish term that refers to cigars with exotic shapes, such

as torpedos, pyramids, perfectos and culebras.

Filler: The individual tobacco leaves used in the body of the cigar. A fine cigar usually contains between two and four different types of filler tobacco.

Flag: An extension of the wrapper leaf shaped to finish the head of a cigar; used instead of a cap. Flags are sometimes tied off in a pigtail or a curly head. A flag is a good indication that a cigar was handmade.

Foot: The end of the cigar you light. In most types of cigars, it is pre-cut, but in torpedos and perfectos, it is sealed.

Gran Corona: A very big cigar;

generally 9 1/4 inches by 47 ring gauge.

Gum: A tasteless vegetable adhesive used to secure the wrapper leaf.

Habano: A designation which, when inscribed on a cigar band, indicates that a cigar is Cuban. (Note: not all Cuban cigars are marked with "Habano" or "Havana.")

Hand: A sheaf of harvested tobacco leaves tied together at the top. Hands are piled together to make a bulk for fermentation.

Handmade: A cigar made entirely by hand with high quality wrapper and long filler. All fine cigars are handmade. Hand-rollers can generally use more delicate wrapper leaves than machines can.

Hand-rolled: All handmade cigars are hand-rolled, but some "hand-rolled" cigars are machine-made up to the point that the wrapper is hand-rolled.

Havana: 1) The capital of Cuba, and the traditional center of manufacturing of Cuban cigars for export. **2)** Cuban cigars are often called "Havanas." **3)** "Havana" is also used as a term to describe tobacco types grown from Cuban seed in places such as the Dominican Republic, Honduras and Nicaragua.

Head: The closed end of the cigar; the end you cut before smoking.

Hot: A term used to describe a cigar that is underfilled and has a quick, loose draw. A hot cigar is likely to taste harsh, instead of mellow.

Humidor: A room or box designed to maintain the proper humidity and temperature for cigar preservation and aging. Humidity should remain around 70 percent, and temperature should stay in the 65°F to 70°F range.

Ligero: An aromatic tobacco which is one of

the three basic types of filler tobacco. The name means "light" in Spanish. "Ligero" is also used to describe light wrapper leaves.

Long filler: A term used to designate filler tobacco that runs the length of fine cigars. Machine-made cigars often use chopped filler.

Machine-made: Cigars made by machine use heavier-weight wrappers and binders and, in many cases, chopped filler, instead of long filler.

Maduro: A shade of wrapper varying from a very dark reddish-brown to almost black. The color results from longer exposure to the sun, a cooking process, or longer fermentation. The word means "ripe" in Spanish.

Mold: 1) A form used to shape the finished bunch for a cigar. It comes in two parts, which are assembled and placed in a press. 2) A potentially damaging fungus that can form on cigars stored at too high a temperature.

Oil: Oil is the mark of a well-humidified cigar. Even well-aged cigars secrete oil at 70-72 percent humidity, the level at which they should be stored.

Oscuro: A black shade of wrapper, darker than maduro, most often Brazilian or Mexican in origin.

"Period of sickness": A time when cigars should not be smoked. Fresh cigars are fine, as are aged ones; but avoid cigars between three months and a year old, during their maturation process.

Plugged: A description of a cigar that has a poor draw.

Puro: A Spanish term used to distinguish a cigar from a cigarette. Modern usage refers to a blend of tobaccos from one country.

Ring gauge: A measurement of the diameter of a cigar, based on 64ths of an inch. A 40 ring gauge cigar is 40/64ths of an inch thick.

Seco: A type of filler tobacco which often contributes aroma and is usually medium-bodied. The word means "dry" in Spanish.

Shade–grown: Wrapper leaves that have been grown under a cheesecloth tent, called a tapado. The filtered sunlight creates a thinner, more elastic leaf.

Smoking time: A 5-inch cigar with a 50 ring gauge, such as a robusto, should provide anywhere from 20 to 30 minutes of smoking pleasure. A double corona— a 7 1/2 inch cigar with a 50 ring gauge—may give over an hour's worth of smoking time. A thinner cigar, such as a Lonsdale, smokes in less time than a cigar with a 50 ring gauge.

Sun–grown: Tobacco grown in direct sunlight, which creates a thicker leaf with thicker veins.

"Totalmente a Mano": Made totally by hand, a description found on cigar boxes. A much better designation than "Hecho a Mano," (made by hand, which can be used for machine-bunched filler that was finished by hand) or "Envuelto a Mano" (packed by hand.)

Tubos: Cigars packed in individual wood, metal or glass tubes to keep them fresh.

Tunneling: The unwelcome phenomenon of having your cigar burn unevenly. To prevent it, rotate your cigar now and then.

Vintage: When a vintage is used for a cigar, it refers to the year the tobacco was harvested, not the year the cigar was made.

Vuelta Abajo: The valley in Cuba that many believe produces the best cigar tobacco in the world.

Volado: A type of filler tobacco, added for its burning qualities.

Wrapper: A high-quality tobacco leaf wrapped around a finished bunch and binder. It is very elastic, and, at its best, unblemished.

ALEXANDRA GRABLEWSKI